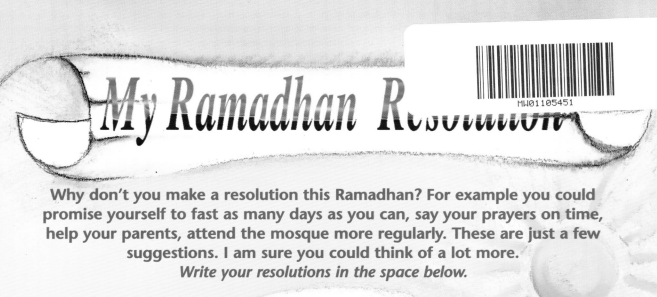

My Ramadhan Resolution

Why don't you make a resolution this Ramadhan? For example you could promise yourself to fast as many days as you can, say your prayers on time, help your parents, attend the mosque more regularly. These are just a few suggestions. I am sure you could think of a lot more.
Write your resolutions in the space below.

Ramadhan Wordsearch

The words are hidden in the Ka'bah. They are written upwards, downwards, across, diagonally, and even backwards. See how quickly you can find them.

TASBIH   EID UL FITR   MERCY   ALLAH   HOLY   FORGIVENESS
REVELATION   WORSHIP   GOOD DEEDS   KINDNESS   FASTING
PRAYERS   DUAS   DATES   QURAN   AMALS   BLESSING
LAYLATUL QADR   FOOD   FRIENDSHIP

Make a *Mobile*

Mobiles come in many forms, from very simple brightly coloured shapes to complicated motorised models. This one is about some of the wonderful creations of Allah, the sun, crescent, star and cloud. You could choose any theme e.g. different flowers and make your own wonderful mobile to give to your friends or hang in your home.

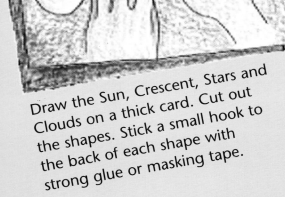

Draw the Sun, Crescent, Stars and Clouds on a thick card. Cut out the shapes. Stick a small hook to the back of each shape with strong glue or masking tape.

Paint the shapes with poster paints. When the paints have thoroughly dried, seal the pieces with two coats of varnish.

To assemble the mobile, cut two pieces of wire about 6 inches each. Attach one piece of wire to the other using short lengths of nylon cord tied through the hooks. Attach other lengths of cord at the ends of the wire and hang the mobile pieces as shown.

The Everlasting Miracle of the Prophet (S.A.W.)

Our Holy Prophet Muhammad (s.a.w.) was born in the month of Rabi-ul-Awwal 570 CE (Christian Era) in the city of Makkah. His father was Abdullah from the great Hashimi tribe and his mother was Amina bint Wahab. Abdullah died a few months before Muhammad (s.a.w.) was born. When Muhammad (S.A.W.) was six years old his mother died. His Grandfather Abdul Muttalib took him into his care. Hardly two years had passed when Abdul Muttalib also passed away. Muhammad then lived with his uncle Abu Talib.

Abu Talib taught Muhammad (s.a.w.) to trade goods. He would take him on his journeys across the desert. Muhammad worked very hard, and soon became known for his hard work and honesty. He started trading goods for a very rich lady called Khadija. Khadija was so impressed by Muhammad's noble character that she asked him to marry her. Muhammad accepted, by this time he was twenty five years old and Khadija was Forty.

The people of Makkah drank alcohol and had no respect towards other people or their properties. They worshiped idols. Muhammad (s.a.w.) was very sad to see how they behaved. When he was about thirty eight years old he started to go to the cave of Hira on Jabal al-nur, the "Mountain of Light" a few miles outside Makkah so that he could pray to Allah in peaceful surroundings. Muhammad spent a long time in the cave. His wife Khadija would visit and send provisions for him. It was on one of these

long stays that on one clear night that Muhammad was visited by angel Jibraeel. Jibraeel said to Muhammad "Read in the name of your Lord who created. He who created man from a clot of clinging blood. Read for your lord is most generous, He who taught the use of the pen, taught man what he knew not." (Al - Alaq) These were the first ayats to be revealed.

When Muhammad came down from the cave of Hira, he told his closest family members and friends about his experiences. The first to accept him as the messenger of

Allah were his wife Khadija and his cousin Ali (a.s.). One day Muhammad invited some of the elders of Makkah to his house. When they came, he asked them " Have you ever heard a lie from me ?" Everyone replied No, you are an honest and truthful man , we have never heard anything but the truth from you.

Muhammad continued, "Then you will know that what I am going to tell you is the Truth; I am the Messenger of Allah. LA ILAHA ILLALLAH MUHAMMAD UR RASULUL-LAH. There is no God but Allah and Muhammad is His Messenger. I invite you to worship one God. You must stop worshipping idols. Some agreed with Muhammad, but many did not wish to stop their old ways. They accused Muhammad of inventing these stories in order to gain popularity They said that any poet could have written it. Muhammad challenged anyone to produce even a single verse to equal the Qur'an which is the true word of Allah. Many poets attempted this task and many worked in groups, but they could not meet this challenge, and through the centuries although now and again people questioned the Qur'an as being the word of Allah, they could not even after fourteen centuries alter or produce a single verse to equal the excellence of the Qur'an.

The Qur'an teaches us many things, it encourages us to think about the world and all its beauties. It tells us about the day of Judgement, when we will see the result of our good and bad deeds. In fact, in the Qur'an we can find answers to any questions that we may have.

The Qur'an was revealed in Arabic, this is why it is recommended to learn the language of the Qur'an. The Qur'an should be read and if possible, its meanings should be understood in the language in which it was revealed. You cannot get a true definition of some of the Arabic words in the Qur'an. For instance, the proper names of certain Prophets have no English equivalents, nor can the names of certain Qur'anic chapters be translated, for example Yaa Seen, Saad, Qaaf, etc.

The Qur'an is divided into 114 sections, each of which is known as "surah" in arabic. These "surahs" consist of about 6205 verses, and all these verses have about 78,000 words. The Qur'an is the living and everlasting miracle of our Holy Prophet (s.a.w.).

The Qur'an is divided into 114 sections. what is each one of these sections known as in Arabic?

In the Qur'an you can find answers to any question that you may have. Can you think of some of the subjects which are covered in the Qur'an?

One of the Surahs was revealed on the night of power. What is this special night known as in Arabic? And which surah was revealed on this night?

When the Prophet (S.A.W.) came down from the mountain, he told his wife about his experiences. Who was the Prophet's (S.A.W.) wife? And who were among the first to accept his message?

An angel brought down the revelation to the Prophet (S.A.W.) What was the name of the angel?

The Qur'an should be read and understood in the language in which it was revealed. Which language was the Qur'an revealed in? And why is it important to learn it?

The Qur'an was revealed in the cave of Hira, on the mountain of Jabal-al-Noor. What does Jabal-al-Noor mean? And why did the Prophet (S.A.W.) go there?

The first revelation to the Prophet (S.A.W.) was, "Read in the name of your Lord who created. He who created. He who created man from a clot of clinging blood. Read, for your Lord is most generous.. He who taught the use of the pen, taught man what he knew not." Do you know which Surah this is from? And can you read it in Arabic

Paper Folding Game

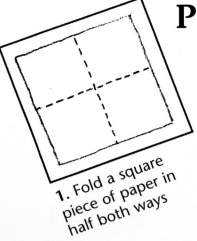

1. Fold a square piece of paper in half both ways

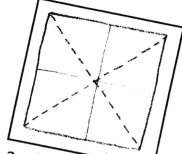

2. Turn the paper over and fold along the diagonals

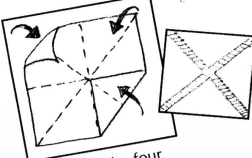

3. Fold all the four corners into the centre

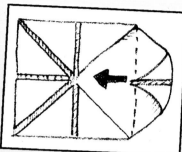

4. Turn the paper over and fold the new corners into the centre

5. Put a number on each of the 8 triangles

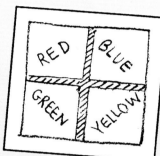

6. Turn it over again and colour each square a different colour

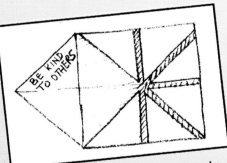

7. Lift each flap of the numbered side and put a message under each number. e.g: (Be kind to others) or (Make a new friend)

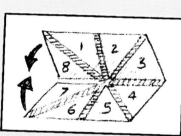

8. Fold it in half with the number on the inside

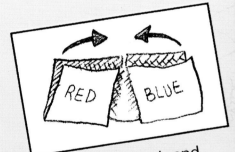

9. Put your thumb and forefinger of each hand into the flaps and press your hands together to make the game close

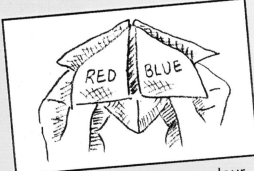

10. Ask a friend to pick a colour, then spell it out opening and closing the game for each letter

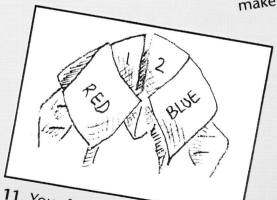

11. Your friend then picks a number from the ones that are showing after spelling out the colour, and under that number will be a message for your friend.

HAVE FUN

Crescent and Stars

Colour this picture in bright colours. There are lots of Crescents and Stars hidden on this page. Have a competition with your friend to see who can find the most in 2 minutes.

One day Prophet Muhammad (S.A.W.) and a group of his followers were passing by a place. They saw an old woman working on her spinning wheel. The Prophet (S.A.W.), after greeting her asked her how she came to believe in Allah.

The old woman let her spinning wheel stop, and then said to him "this spinning wheel stops spinning if no one turns it, What about the wonders of the universe. Who changes the days into nights and nights into days? Who changes the four seasons? Who created the land, and the seas? Who created the sun so bright? and the moon so high up in the sky? Who put the breath into us and gave us life? And who can take it away in an instant?

Only Allah can do all this. It is Allah who created the days so that we may go about our daily lives, remembering our maker in all that we do. He made the nights so that we may rest. He made some special, like the night of Qadr, when he revealed the Qur'an to guide us. He created the four seasons so that we may see the miracle of life. In spring a beautiful flower is born and grows

T I O N

stronger through summer and then in autumn it withers and finally in winter it dies. And then once again by the miracle of Allah it comes up in spring. This is a lesson to us. We, just like the flower go through the seasons of life. We must try to do good in the summer of our lives when we are strong. And just like the flower, we too will come up again on the day of Judgement, when we have to answer for all our deeds. He created the land for us to live on, and grow the food that we need. He created the sea. He made the sun to give life to living things. He created the moon so that we may know the beginning of a new month, like this holy month of Ramadhan, and then at the end of it the excitement of waiting for the new moon to mark the day of Eid. A very happy Eid to you all. O children of the world may all your wishes and dreams come true. He put the breath into us and gave us life. and he can take it away in an instant.

The Prophet (S.A.W.) turned to his companions and said " This old woman really believes in the existence of Allah You too must have a strong belief in Allah. See the wonders that Allah has created and be thankful for them".

Feed the Birds

Feed the birds in your garden. It is particularly important to feed them in the winter. Put the food on your bird table and then watch another one of Allah's wonderful creations up close!

Make a Bird Cake

You Need:
A bowl of very hot water
A cake tin with a removable bottom
1cup of hard vegetable fat
Any of the following:
Food scraps (e.g. dried fruit, plain breakfast cereal, grated cheese, maize, millet, biscuit and cake crumbs) or bird seed from the pet store.

1. Mix all the ingredients together (except the fat) together.

2. Warm the fat until it is soft, pour over the mixture and stir well until everything is coated.

3. Press the mixture into the cake tin. place a plate over the top and put something heavy on top of that. Put it in the fridge for at least a day.

4. Push the cake out of the tin and put it on the bird table.

Remember the cake is for the birds! They'll love the taste, you won't!

Water is Important

Birds need water to drink and bathe in. You can put out a dish of water all year round. Change the water every day and in the winter put a ball in the water to prevent it from freezing.

WARNING!

Don't use anything very salty. Don't give bird cake or peanut in the spring. There is plenty of food around then and their babies might choke on nuts.

Make a Bird Feeder

You Need:
A plastic bottle, String, 3 Pieces of thin wood, Unsalted Peanuts

1. Make 2 holes on opposites sides of the bottle for string to hang it up

2. Make holes for the pieces of wood.

3. Push the wood through the holes for the birds to sit on.

4. Make some slits into the bottle. Take care not to cut the slits too large otherwise the peanuts will spill through.

5. Fill the bottle with peanuts. Screw the top on and hang it up.

Fill
in the Blanks

There is no God but ...., and .... is His messenger.

Muslims pray .... a day.

The .... is the call for prayers.

The Prophet (S.A.W.) asked .... to call for prayers for the first time.

We face the .... for our ....

The Ka'abah is in .... in Saudi Arabia.

.... is the month of fasting. We fast from dawn to ....

We are recommended to break our fast with ....

Ramadhan is the .... month in the Islamic calendar.

There are .... months in the Islamic calendar.

.... is the first month in the Islamic calendar.

The .... was revealed in the month of ....

It was revealed in the cave of .... on the mountain of ....

The Qur'an was revealed to the .... (S.A.W.) when he was .... years old.

The Qur'an was brought down to .... us, and keep us on the right ....

The Qur'an was revealed on the night of ....

The night of power is known as .... in Arabic.

Eid-ul-Fitr is celebrated at the end of ....

Zakat-ul-Fitr should be paid at the end of .... before Eid prayers.

Our holy Prophet (S.A.W.) was born in the month of ....

The Qur'an is the everlasting .... of our .... (S.A.W.)

Make your own Tasbih

Before you take your old magazines to the recycling skip, take out some of the most colourful pages and make some beads for your very own Tasbih.

Cut a piece of colourful paper into long strips, slightly wider at one end.

Starting from the widest end of the paper strip, roll each one around your stick or knitting needle.

Dab some glue on the underside of the paper, to hold it all in place. you could use PVA or glue stick.

To make the Tasbih, thread through 34 beads onto a length of string. (Dental floss or fishing tackle is great for this as it is very strong!) Knot the ends together.

You could add beads made from strips of foil, as this will add sparkle to your Tasbih.

Paint your beads with PVA glue to make them stronger and shiny too.

Experiment with different types of paper to create different types of bead effects. Tissue paper, sugar paper and even newspaper can be used and look great.

Laylat-ul-Qadr

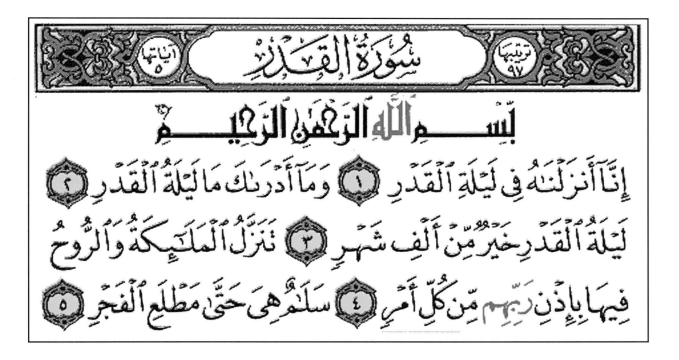

Bismillahir Rahmanir Rahiim.....In the name of Allah, Most Gracious, Most Merciful.

Innaa anzalnaahu fii laylati-l qadr.....We have indeed revealed it (the Qur'an) in the night of Qadr.

Wa maa Adraaka maa Laylatu-l qadr.....What will explain to you what the Night of Qadr is?

Laylatu-l-qadri khayrun(m)min alfi shahr.....The night of Qadr is better than a thousand months.

Tanazzalu-l malaaa'ikatu wa-r ruuhu fiihaa bi idhni rabbihim min Kulli Amr.....On this night the angels and the holy spirits come down by the permission of their Lord, with (decrees) of all affairs.

Salaamun hiya hatta matla'i-l fajr.....Peace!...through the night until the rise of dawn.

It is on the night of Qadr that the Greatest miracle ever witnessed by mankind (the Qur'an) was brought down. There is special significance about prayers on this night. The angels come down from the heavens to bring us special blessings and peace from Allah for those who spend this night in prayers. It is promised that whoever prays to Allah for forgiveness on this night, their sins shall be forgiven. The actual night has been kept a secret, so that we may spend our time in prayers to Allah as much as we can. This special night of Qadr is said to be in one of the last days of Ramadhan.

MAZE

Why don't you amaze yourself by seeing how quickly you can find your way to the Mosque.

Chocolate Dips

You can put chocolate fruits and nuts into cup cake cases and give them to your family and friends as a special Eid gift.

What you need:

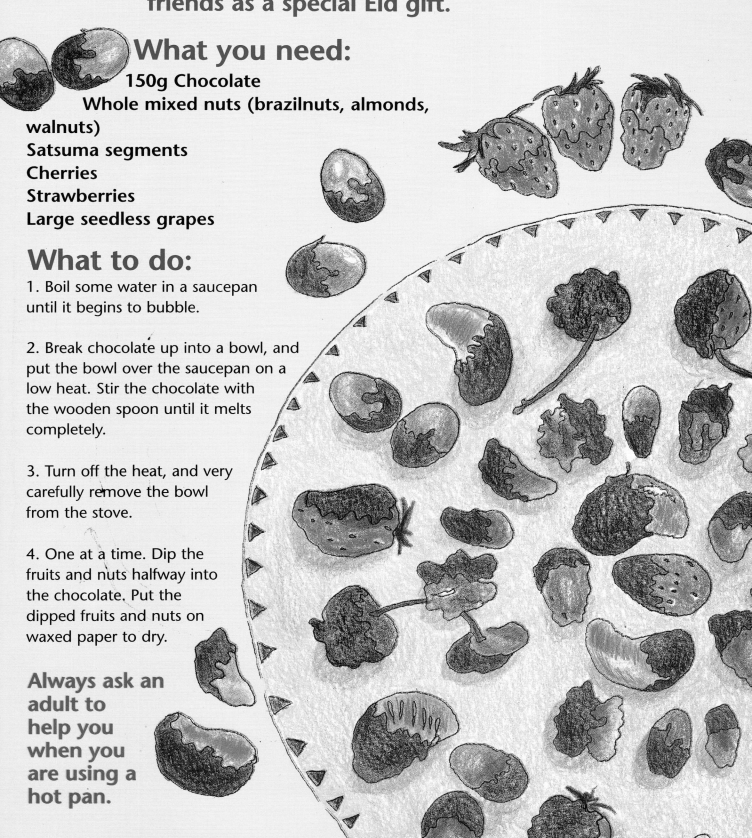

150g Chocolate
Whole mixed nuts (brazilnuts, almonds, walnuts)
Satsuma segments
Cherries
Strawberries
Large seedless grapes

What to do:

1. Boil some water in a saucepan until it begins to bubble.

2. Break chocolate up into a bowl, and put the bowl over the saucepan on a low heat. Stir the chocolate with the wooden spoon until it melts completely.

3. Turn off the heat, and very carefully remove the bowl from the stove.

4. One at a time. Dip the fruits and nuts halfway into the chocolate. Put the dipped fruits and nuts on waxed paper to dry.

Always ask an adult to help you when you are using a hot pan.

Make Your Own Eid Decorations

Paper Chains

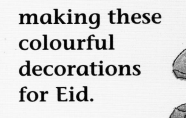

To make paper chains, cut strips of thin coloured paper about 1in X 6in. Fold one strip into a loop and glue the ends together. Thread the next strip through and stick into a second loop as shown. Continue in this way to make a long chain.

Have lots of fun making these colourful decorations for Eid.

Bows

1. To make beautiful bows. Cut a length of coloured tissue paper about 18in long. Fold both ends in the centre and glue them in place.

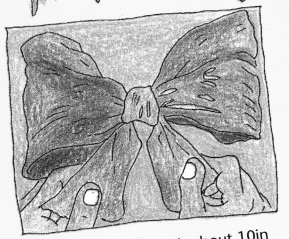

2. Cut a second length about 10in long. Pinch the original paper in the centre and tie the second paper around it to form a bow. You could make lots of different coloured bows.

1. Always remember to cover work surfaces with newspapers or an old cloth.

2. Never leave sharp instruments like scissors or craft knives around where small children can reach them.

3. Always put the tops back on the glue to prevent them from drying out.

Colour this picture of the Al-Aqsa Mosque in Jerusalem.

Jerusalem is the third holy city of Islam. It was here that our Prophet Muhammad
(S.A.W.) was lifted up to the heavens on Buraq.

Make your own *Block Printing* Eid Cards

Always ask anadult for help while using a sharp instruments

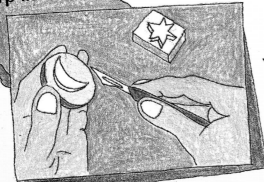

You can make wonderful designs using blocks cut from potatoes. For longer lasting blocks you can use erasers. You can use paints or an ink pad.

1. Cut a potato in half, making sure that the cut surface is flat so that the design will print evenly onto paper. Cut your design into the potato. You can also use the same process to make blocks from erasers.

2. Mix some paint with a little water and dab it on to the block with a paint brush. Press the block carefully on to a card and lift it up again.

3. Fold the card and write your message inside

Fold a strip of card alternately backward and forward, and write your message as shown.

These are just a few ideas that you can use for making Eid cards with block printing. I am sure you can think of many more exciting ideas.